DISTINCTIVE SOUTH FLORIDA BIRDS

Roseate Spoonbill
Platalea ajaja
To 32 in. (80 cm)
Bill is flattened at the tip.

Everglades Snail Kite
Rostrhamus sociabilis
To 19 in. (48 cm)
Feeds almost exclusively on apple snails.

Limpkin
Aramus guarauna
To 28 in. (70 cm)

Purple Gallinule
Porphyrio martinicus
To 13 in. (33 cm)

Magnificent Frigatebird
Fregata magnificens
To 40 in. (1 m)
Note huge wingspan and a forked tail.

Wood Stork
Mycteria americana
To 4 ft. (1.2 m)
Dark head is naked.

Mangrove Cuckoo
Coccyzus minor
To 12 in. (30 cm)

Florida Scrub-Jay
Aphelocoma coerulescens
To 13 in. (33 cm)

Reddish Egret
Egretta rufescens
To 30 in. (75 cm)

FORT MYERS & NAPLES WILDLIFE

A Folding Pocket Guide to Familiar Animals of Southwestern Florida

FORT MYERS & NAPLES WILDLIFE – A Folding Pocket Guide to Familiar Animals   Kavanagh/Leung

BUTTERFLIES

Spicebush Swallowtail
Papilio troilus
To 4.5 in. (11 cm)

Zebra Swallowtail
Eurytides marcellus
To 3.5 in. (9 cm)

Eastern Tiger Swallowtail
Papilio glaucus
To 6 in. (15 cm)

Cabbage White
Pieris rapae
To 2 in. (5 cm)
One of the most common butterflies.

Red Admiral
Vanessa atalanta
To 2.5 in. (6 cm)

Orange Sulphur
Colias eurytheme
To 2.5 in. (6 cm)
Note prominent forewing spot.

Mourning Cloak
Nymphalis antiopa
To 3.5 in. (9 cm)
Emerges during the first spring thaw.

Monarch
Danaus plexippus
To 4 in. (10 cm)

Orange-barred Sulphur
Phoebis philea
To 3 in. (8 cm)
Note broad orange bar on forewings.

Buckeye
Junonia coenia
To 2.5 in. (6 cm)

Red-spotted Purple
Limenitis arthemis astyanax
To 3 in. (8 cm)

Southern Dogface
Zerene cesonia
To 2.5 in. (6 cm)
Note poodle-head pattern on forewings.

White Peacock
Anartia jatrophae
To 2.5 in. (6 cm)

Gulf Fritillary
Agraulis vanillae
To 3 in. (8 cm)
Underwings are covered with metallic silver spots.

Queen
Danaus gilippus
To 3.5 in. (9 cm)

Zebra Longwing
Heliconius charithonia
To 3.5 in. (9 cm)

REPTILES

American Alligator
Alligator mississippiensis
To 20 ft. (6 m)
Florida's state reptile.

Gopher Tortoise
Gopherus polyphemus
To 14 in. (35 cm)

Snapping Turtle
Chelydra serpentina
To 18 in. (45 cm)
Note large head and long tail.

Southeastern Five-lined Skink
Plestiodon inexpectatus
To 9 in. (23 cm)
Smooth, glossy scales. Has five narrow light stripes down back.

Brown Anole
Anolis sagrei
To 9 in. (23 cm)
Introduced species.

Green Anole
Anolis carolinensis
To 8 in. (20 cm)
Green lizard has a wedge-shaped snout.

Six-lined Racerunner
Aspidoscelis sexlineata
To 11 in. (28 cm)
Speedy lizard has 6-7 yellowish stripes on its back. Scales are not shiny.

Mediterranean Gecko
Hemidactylus turcicus To 5 in. (13 cm)
Has unwebbed feet and large toe pads.

Florida Water Snake
Nerodia fasciata pictiventris
To 42 in. (1.1 m)
Has black, brown or red crossbands.

Corn Snake
Pantherophis guttatus
To 6 ft. (1.8 m)
Told by black-bordered, red blotches.

Pigmy Rattlesnake
Sistrurus miliarius barbouri
To 31 in. (78 cm)
Small venomous rattlesnake.

Southern Black Racer
Coluber constrictor priapus
To 6 ft. (1.8 m)
Dark snake has a white chin.

Eastern Coral Snake
Micrurus fulvius To 4 ft. (1.2 m)
Venomous.

Eastern Diamondback Rattlesnake
Crotalus adamanteus To 8 ft. (2.4 m)
Large venomous snake has dark, diamond-shaped blotches down its back.

Cottonmouth
Agkistrodon piscivorus
To 6 ft. (1.8 m)
Large poisonous water snake has a spade-shaped head.

MAMMALS

Eastern Gray Squirrel
Sciurus carolinensis
To 20 in. (50 cm)

Mangrove Squirrel
Sciurus niger avicennia
To 28 in. (70 cm)
Note large size. Color is variable.

Nine-banded Armadillo
Dasypus novemcinctus
To 32 in. (80 cm)

Virginia Opossum
Didelphis virginiana
To 40 in. (1 m)

Marsh Rabbit
Sylvilagus palustris
To 18 in. (45 cm)

Eastern Cottontail
Sylvilagus floridanus
To 18 in. (45 cm)

Striped Skunk
Mephitis mephitis To 30 in. (75 cm)

Common Gray Fox
Urocyon cinereoargenteus
To 3.5 ft. (1.1 m)

Common Raccoon
Procyon lotor
To 40 in. (1 m)

Long-tailed Weasel
Mustela frenata
To 21 in. (53 cm)

Northern River Otter
Lontra canadensis
To 52 in. (1.3 m)

Bobcat
Lynx rufus
To 4 ft. (1.2 m)
Dark snake has a white chin.

Black Bear
Ursus americanus
To 6 ft. (1.8 m)

White-tailed Deer
Odocoileus virginianus
To 7 ft. (2.1 m)

MAMMALS

Bottlenose Dolphin
Tursiops truncatus
To 12 ft. (3.6 m)
Florida's state saltwater mammal.

Manatee
Trichechus manatus
To 13 ft. (3.9 m)
Florida's state marine mammal.

WATERBIRDS AND NEARSHORE BIRDS

Mallard
Anas platyrhynchos To 28 in. (70 cm)

Wood Duck
Aix sponsa To 20 in. (50 cm)

Red-breasted Merganser
Mergus serrator To 27 in. (68 cm)
Note thin bill and prominent head crest.

Blue-winged Teal
Spatula discors To 16 in. (40 cm)

White Ibis
Eudocimus albus
To 28 in. (70 cm)
Adult   Juvenile

Green Heron
Butorides virescens
To 22 in. (55 cm)

Black-crowned Night-Heron
Nycticorax nycticorax
To 28 in. (70 cm)

Great Egret
Ardea alba
To 38 in. (95 cm)
Note yellow bill and black feet.

Snowy Egret
Egretta thula
To 26 in. (65 cm)
Note black bill and yellow feet.

American Coot
Fulica americana
To 16 in. (40 cm)

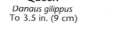

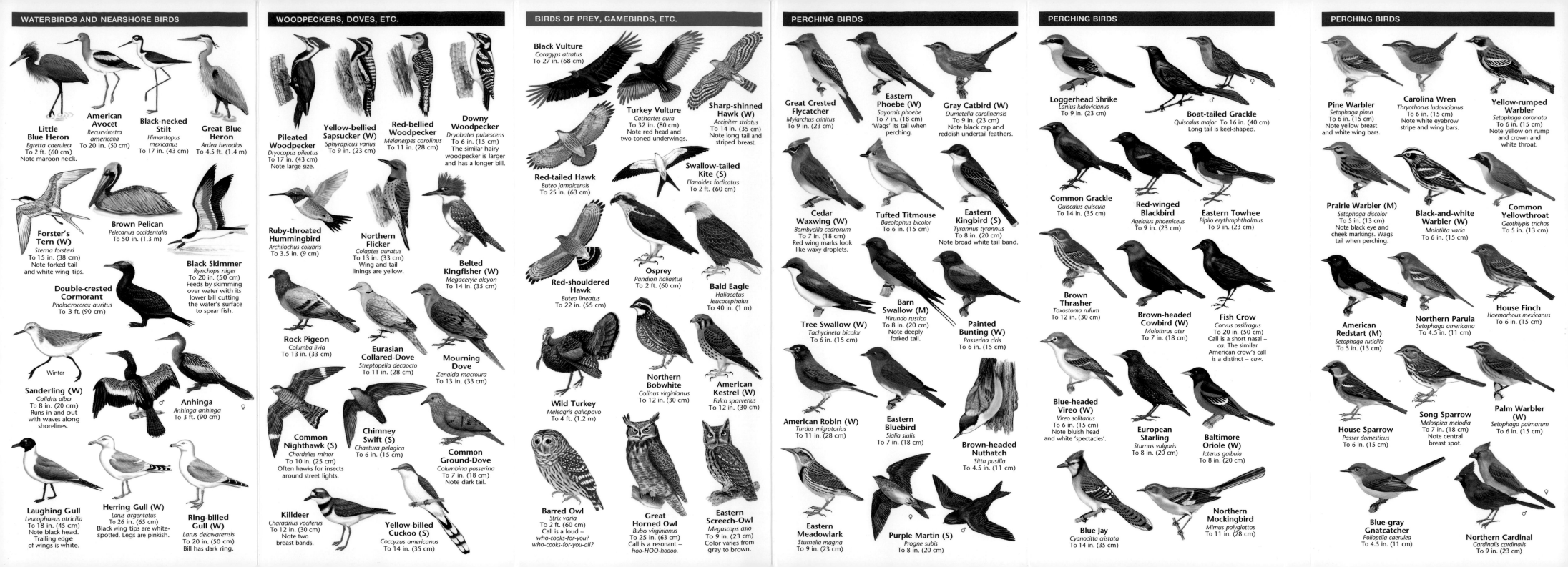

WATERBIRDS AND NEARSHORE BIRDS

Little Blue Heron
Egretta caerulea
To 2 ft. (60 cm)
Note maroon neck.

American Avocet
Recurvirostra americana
To 20 in. (50 cm)

Black-necked Stilt
Himantopus mexicanus
To 17 in. (43 cm)

Great Blue Heron
Ardea herodias
To 4.5 ft. (1.4 m)

Forster's Tern (W)
Sterna forsteri
To 15 in. (38 cm)
Note forked tail and white wing tips.

Brown Pelican
Pelecanus occidentalis
To 50 in. (1.3 m)

Black Skimmer
Rynchops niger
To 20 in. (50 cm)
Feeds by skimming over water with its lower bill cutting the water's surface to spear fish.

Double-crested Cormorant
Phalacrocorax auritus
To 3 ft. (90 cm)

Winter

Sanderling (W)
Calidris alba
To 8 in. (20 cm)
Runs in and out with waves along shorelines.

Anhinga
Anhinga anhinga
To 3 ft. (90 cm)

Laughing Gull
Leucophaeus atricilla
To 18 in. (45 cm)
Note black head. Trailing edge of wings is white.

Herring Gull (W)
Larus argentatus
To 26 in. (65 cm)
Black wing tips are white-spotted. Legs are pinkish.

Ring-billed Gull (W)
Larus delawarensis
To 20 in. (50 cm)
Bill has dark ring.

WOODPECKERS, DOVES, ETC.

Pileated Woodpecker
Dryocopus pileatus
To 17 in. (43 cm)
Note large size.

Yellow-bellied Sapsucker (W)
Sphyrapicus varius
To 9 in. (23 cm)

Red-bellied Woodpecker
Melanerpes carolinus
To 11 in. (28 cm)

Downy Woodpecker
Dryobates pubescens
To 6 in. (15 cm)
The similar hairy woodpecker is larger and has a longer bill.

Ruby-throated Hummingbird
Archilochus colubris
To 3.5 in. (9 cm)

Northern Flicker
Colaptes auratus
To 13 in. (33 cm)
Wing and tail linings are yellow.

Belted Kingfisher (W)
Megaceryle alcyon
To 14 in. (35 cm)

Rock Pigeon
Columba livia
To 13 in. (33 cm)

Eurasian Collared-Dove
Streptopelia decaocto
To 11 in. (28 cm)

Mourning Dove
Zenaida macroura
To 13 in. (33 cm)

Common Nighthawk (S)
Chordeiles minor
To 10 in. (25 cm)
Often hawks for insects around street lights.

Chimney Swift (S)
Chaetura pelagica
To 6 in. (15 cm)

Common Ground-Dove
Columbina passerina
To 7 in. (18 cm)
Note dark tail.

Killdeer
Charadrius vociferus
To 12 in. (30 cm)
Note two breast bands.

Yellow-billed Cuckoo (S)
Coccyzus americanus
To 14 in. (35 cm)

BIRDS OF PREY, GAMEBIRDS, ETC.

Black Vulture
Coragyps atratus
To 27 in. (68 cm)

Turkey Vulture
Cathartes aura
To 32 in. (80 cm)
Note red head and two-toned underwings.

Sharp-shinned Hawk (W)
Accipiter striatus
To 14 in. (35 cm)
Note long tail and striped breast.

Red-tailed Hawk
Buteo jamaicensis
To 25 in. (63 cm)

Swallow-tailed Kite (S)
Elanoides forficatus
To 2 ft. (60 cm)

Red-shouldered Hawk
Buteo lineatus
To 22 in. (55 cm)

Osprey
Pandion haliaetus
To 2 ft. (60 cm)

Bald Eagle
Haliaeetus leucocephalus
To 40 in. (1 m)

Wild Turkey
Meleagris gallopavo
To 4 ft. (1.2 m)

Northern Bobwhite
Colinus virginianus
To 12 in. (30 cm)

American Kestrel (W)
Falco sparverius
To 12 in. (30 cm)

Barred Owl
Strix varia
To 2 ft. (60 cm)
Call is a loud –
who-cooks-for-you?
who-cooks-for-you-all?

Great Horned Owl
Bubo virginianus
To 25 in. (63 cm)
Call is a resonant –
hoo-HOO-hoooo.

Eastern Screech-Owl
Megascops asio
To 9 in. (23 cm)
Color varies from gray to brown.

PERCHING BIRDS

Great Crested Flycatcher
Myiarchus crinitus
To 9 in. (23 cm)

Eastern Phoebe (W)
Sayornis phoebe
To 7 in. (18 cm)
'Wags' its tail when perching.

Gray Catbird (W)
Dumetella carolinensis
To 9 in. (23 cm)
Note black cap and reddish undertail feathers.

Cedar Waxwing (W)
Bombycilla cedrorum
To 7 in. (18 cm)
Red wing marks look like waxy droplets.

Tufted Titmouse
Baeolophus bicolor
To 6 in. (15 cm)

Eastern Kingbird (S)
Tyrannus tyrannus
To 8 in. (20 cm)
Note broad white tail band.

Tree Swallow (W)
Tachycineta bicolor
To 6 in. (15 cm)

Barn Swallow (M)
Hirundo rustica
To 8 in. (20 cm)
Note deeply forked tail.

Painted Bunting (S)
Passerina ciris
To 6 in. (15 cm)

American Robin (W)
Turdus migratorius
To 11 in. (28 cm)

Eastern Bluebird
Sialia sialis
To 7 in. (18 cm)

Brown-headed Nuthatch
Sitta pusilla
To 4.5 in. (11 cm)

Eastern Meadowlark
Sturnella magna
To 9 in. (23 cm)

Purple Martin (S)
Progne subis
To 8 in. (20 cm)

PERCHING BIRDS

Loggerhead Shrike
Lanius ludovicianus
To 9 in. (23 cm)

Boat-tailed Grackle
Quiscalus major To 16 in. (40 cm)
Long tail is keel-shaped.

Common Grackle
Quiscalus quiscula
To 14 in. (35 cm)

Red-winged Blackbird
Agelaius phoeniceus
To 9 in. (23 cm)

Eastern Towhee
Pipilo erythrophthalmus
To 9 in. (23 cm)

Brown Thrasher
Toxostoma rufum
To 12 in. (30 cm)

Brown-headed Cowbird (W)
Molothrus ater
To 7 in. (18 cm)

Fish Crow
Corvus ossifragus
To 20 in. (50 cm)
Call is a short nasal –
ca. The similar American crow's call is a distinct – caw.

Blue-headed Vireo (W)
Vireo solitarius
To 6 in. (15 cm)
Note bluish head and white 'spectacles'.

European Starling
Sturnus vulgaris
To 8 in. (20 cm)

Baltimore Oriole (W)
Icterus galbula
To 8 in. (20 cm)

Blue Jay
Cyanocitta cristata
To 14 in. (35 cm)

Northern Mockingbird
Mimus polyglottos
To 11 in. (28 cm)

PERCHING BIRDS

Pine Warbler
Setophaga pinus
To 6 in. (15 cm)
Note yellow breast and white wing bars.

Carolina Wren
Thryothorus ludovicianus
To 6 in. (15 cm)

Yellow-rumped Warbler
Setophaga coronata
To 6 in. (15 cm)
Note yellow on rump and crown and white throat.

Prairie Warbler (M)
Setophaga discolor
To 5 in. (13 cm)
Note black eye and cheek markings. Wags tail when perching.

Black-and-white Warbler (W)
Mniotilta varia
To 6 in. (15 cm)

Common Yellowthroat
Geothlypis trichas
To 5 in. (13 cm)

American Redstart (M)
Setophaga ruticilla
To 5 in. (13 cm)

Northern Parula
Setophaga americana
To 4.5 in. (11 cm)

House Finch
Haemorhous mexicanus
To 6 in. (15 cm)

House Sparrow
Passer domesticus
To 6 in. (15 cm)

Song Sparrow (W)
Melospiza melodia
To 7 in. (18 cm)
Note central breast spot.

Palm Warbler (W)
Setophaga palmarum
To 6 in. (15 cm)

Blue-gray Gnatcatcher
Polioptila caerulea
To 4.5 in. (11 cm)

Northern Cardinal
Cardinalis cardinalis
To 9 in. (23 cm)